Homemade Treats for Happy, Healthy Dogs

Cheryl Gianfrancesco

CONTENTS

Introduction

When Kooper arrived home, he was a fuzzy ball of fur eager to explore his new home. He was immediately the king of my household. I did everything a new pet owner is supposed to do: I took him to a veterinarian, who gave him all the necessary vaccinations, and I fed him what I thought were the best premium dog food and treats available from specialty pet stores. I didn't know anything about pet nutrition, but I assumed that the companies making dog food knew what was healthful for a dog. If not, they wouldn't be in business, right?

A few months later, Kooper began to vomit and have uncontrollable diarrhea. I immediately took him to the veterinarian, who told me that Kooper was having a reaction to the dog food and treats he was eating. He prescribed a food that was easily digestible and banned treats of any kind from Kooper's diet.

Soon after Kooper began eating the new dog food, he was back to his old self. When I contacted his veterinarian with the good news, he told me that Kooper would have to eat that way for the rest of his life. I was crushed! I would never be able to pamper my dog; I would never be able to give him a treat as a reward for good behavior or just because he looked at me in that loving way with those big brown eyes.

I refused to believe that Kooper was the only dog in the world who couldn't tolerate to his food and treats, and I began to do some research. Most of my local library's books on dog health dedicated only a page or two to dog nutrition, but that was enough. Armed with all the information about nutrition that I needed, I searched pet stores and read endless lists of dog-food and dog-treat ingredients, hoping to find Kooper the best food and treats available. I couldn't pronounce, much less recognize, more than half the ingredients listed on the labels of the brands I picked up. I was very frustrated: The time I had spent looking for commercial treats that wouldn't aggravate Kooper's sensitive gut was wasted.

The Big Decision

Having found no healthful dog treats in the stores, I began to think about baking my own treats for Kooper. I looked and looked for recipes. Unfortunately, all the ones I found were loaded with salt, sugar, and animal fat — not the most nutritious ingredients. Finally, I decided to develop my own recipes using all-natural ingredients.

I began slowly, not sure if Kooper would have bad reactions to any of the ingredients I chose. I wasn't even sure if he would like how they tasted. To my surprise, he loved the treats, and he had no adverse reactions to any of them. I then slowly began to expand the range of natural products I was using. The results were the same: no negative reactions, and a very happy dog.

Some of my friends had dogs with similar dietary problems. I gave them some of my homemade treats for their dogs to try; like Kooper, they had no negative reactions and wanted more. The treats were a hit even with dogs that didn't have health issues!

I believe variety is important, so I continue to develop more and more recipes for nutritious, all-natural homemade dog treats. I enjoy these baking projects, and I love seeing Kooper munch on treats that I know are good for him.

Why Bake Your Own?

Have you ever looked at the list of ingredients on a box of dog treats? What color are the ones you give your dog — orange, because they're "cheese-flavored"? Or reddish brown, because they're supposed to taste like liver? Now consider this: Have you ever seen a "use by" date or an expiration date on a dog-food product? It seems like this food can last virtually forever! There's no way to know how long your dog's treats have been sitting on the shelf.

Until Kooper got sick, I never checked labels or thought about all the additives and artificial ingredients in most dog foods. I just bought them because I liked the way they looked, or I'd seen a commercial for them on television, or they had been on sale, never thinking much about their nutritional content or lack thereof. And I certainly never wondered about how old those packaged goods might be when I bought them.

I've learned a lot since then. And as far as I'm concerned, you should avoid any pet-food ingredients with the words *by-products* and *meal* on the label. Generally speaking, these are food-processing by-products that humans will not consume. Other undesirable — even potentially harmful — ingredients include chemicals, preservatives, artificial flavorings, and artificial colorings. Many of these substances are unpronounceable and unrecognizable to the average consumer, and none are safe for sensitive stomachs.

Proper nutrition and regular veterinary care are the two key ingredients for a healthy, happy dog. And I believe that if everyone was aware of the quality of ingredients in store-bought dog food and treats, more people would cook for their pets. The recipes in this bulletin include high-quality ingredients, no fillers, no added colors, and no preservatives or artificial flavorings — and best of all, they're easy to prepare. Making homemade dog treats is one way to take control of your dog's health — and to do something special for your best friend.

Alternatives to Baked Treats

When you don't have time to bake for your dog, there are many other healthful foods you can offer as treats. Choose dried dates and dried apricots (both without added sugar), baby carrots, and apple slices. Be sure to remove any seeds, and wash fruits and vegetables well to remove pesticides and preservatives before feeding these foods to your dog. Keep portions small. And remember, any time you give your dog new foods, watch for signs of adverse reactions (see page 6).

When You Must Buy Commercial Products

While I'm a strong advocate of making your own all-natural dog treats, I realize you may not always have the time, or the desire, to do so. If you must purchase dog treats or dog food, be sure to choose products whose primary ingredients (the first few listed on the label) are whole foods, such as chicken, beef, lamb, brown rice, whole wheat, barley, and oats. By-products, meal, corn, and any unpronounceable ingredients, if present, should be near the end of the list of contents. The best treats have a short, simple list of ingredients.

Many pet owners today are concerned about their pet's diet, prompting the development of more healthful, all-natural products. There are plenty of pet specialty stores and Internet resources that offer a wide selection of dog treats and dog foods. Don't be fooled by the packaging or the price — read the ingredient lists and make educated choices.

Tips and Tricks for the Best Treats

Whether you're a seasoned cook or a novice, baking for your dog can be both rewarding and challenging. As I've experimented, I've learned the following things that make the baking easier for me, and more healthful for Kooper and other dogs:

- Be as creative as you like with these recipes! Add different ingredients that you think your dog may like (but remember to try only one new ingredient at a time so that you can monitor if your dog has any kind of reaction).
- Most of these recipes call for whole-wheat flour, but if your dog cannot tolerate it or you have none in the house, you can use unbleached white flour. If your dog is allergic, try an alternative, such as gluten-free mix that's sold in health food stores.
- Many peanut butters contain lots of sugar and salt. In recipes that call for peanut butter, use the all-natural, no-salt- and no-sugar-added type, available at most large grocery stores.
- Do *not* use ingredients that contain any traces of chocolate, onions, grapes, raisins, seeds from fruits, or caffeine. These ingredients are harmful and, depending on the amount consumed, can be fatal to your dog. (Carob, found in health-food stores, is a nutritious chocolate substitute.)
- Use organic ingredients, if they're available to you. You can find organic products at farmer's markets and natural-food stores.
- If your dough does not seem firm enough, add some flour, 1 tablespoon at a time, mixing or kneading it in until the dough is firm. If the dough is too stiff and crumbly, add water, 1 tablespoon at a time.
- If the dough sticks to your rolling pin as you're rolling it out, pat flour onto the surface of the rolling pin.
- Make it fun! Use a variety of shaped cookie cutters for the treats. (I have not included yields for these recipes, because the quantity depends on the size of the cookie cutter used.)
- Baking times can vary. Check the treats periodically during baking to make sure they're not cooking more quickly than expected.
- Be sure the treats are cooled completely before you serve any to your dog.

Testing for Food Intolerances and Allergies

Just like humans, dogs can have food intolerances or allergies. A food intolerance is when a pet does not tolerate an ingredient, such as dietary fat or fiber. A food allergy is an immune reaction to a specific dietary protein or antigen. The signs of a food intolerance and a food allergy can be similar, with both potentially causing gastrointestinal disturbances such as vomiting and diarrhea. True food allergies can also manifest in the skin, as itching or irritation.

If your dog has never been exposed to an ingredient, I suggest starting with a simple recipe that has few ingredients.

1. Give your dog a small piece of the treat — less than half — and wait a few hours, watching the dog for any sign of food intolerance or allergic reaction. This can be as simple as scratching more than usual or as dramatic as vomiting, swelling of face and/or throat, and diarrhea. If any of these more dramatic symptoms develop, contact your veterinarian immediately.

2. If no reaction occurs, give your dog the rest of the treat and wait a few hours, watching for a reaction. If one does occur, do not give your dog any more of that particular treat. Make note of which ingredients were used in the treat, and try making and testing different versions, keeping track of which ingredients are used and which recipes cause a negative response.

Some allergic reactions may not manifest immediately. Therefore, don't introduce more than one new ingredient in a week. With time and patience, you should be able to isolate the ingredients to which your dog is intolerant or allergic.

My Favorite Recipes

Most of these recipes will take less than 15 minutes to mix the ingredients, cut the cookies, and place them on a baking sheet. Most of the ingredients are inexpensive, and you'll find them at your local grocery or health-food store. Almost all of them are simple, one-bowl recipes.

If you're just beginning to bake treats for your dog, start with the simpler recipes, such as Peanut Butter Biscuits (page 7), Apple-

Oatmeal Cookies (page 20), and Tempting Cheese Circles (page 25), and test for food intolerance or allergies as described above. These recipes will also help you determine your dog's likes and dislikes.

Note: While these treats are healthful for your dog, they are still treats. They are not intended to be a complete diet and should make up no more than 10 percent of your dog's total daily calories.

Recipe Yields

The yield of any particular recipe will depend on the size of the cookie cutter you use. As a rule of thumb, if you use a 2-inch-diameter circular cutter, every 2 cups of flour in a recipe equate to about 3 dozen cookies. For example, a recipe calling for 4 cups of flour will yield about 6 dozen cookies, and a recipe calling for 6 cups of flour will yield about 9 dozen.

Nut-and-Seed Nibbles

Essential fatty acids, found in nuts and seeds, help keep your dog energized and ensure a shiny, healthy coat.

PEANUT BUTTER BISCUITS

    4 **cups whole-wheat flour**
    2 **cups quick-cooking oats**
 2½ **cups warm water**
   ½ **cup all-natural peanut butter (no sugar or salt added)**
   ¼ **cup carob chips (available at health food stores)**

1. Preheat the oven to 350°F. In a large bowl, combine all ingredients; mix well.

2. On a lightly floured surface, knead the dough until it is firm. If the dough is too sticky, add warm water, 1 tablespoon at a time, while continuing to knead.

3. Roll the dough to a ¼-inch thickness. Cut with the cookie cutter of your choice. Transfer biscuits to a baking sheet.

4. Bake the biscuits for 40 minutes. Turn off the heat and let the biscuits stand in the oven until hard, 1 to 2 hours.

PEANUT BUTTER AND BANANA TREATS

   3 cups whole-wheat flour
   ½ cup wheat germ
   1 cup water
   ¼ cup all-natural peanut butter
      (no sugar or salt added)
   1 egg
   1 banana, mashed

1. Preheat the oven to 350°F. In a large bowl, combine all ingredients; mix well.

2. On a floured surface, knead the dough until it is firm.

3. Roll the dough to a ¼-inch thickness. Cut with the cookie cutter of your choice. Transfer cookies to a baking sheet.

4. Bake for 45 to 55 minutes, or until the cookies are dry and firm to touch. Turn off the heat; let the cookies stand in the oven until hard, 1 to 2 hours.

NUTTY BONES

   2 cups whole-wheat flour
   ¼ cup wheat germ
   ¼ cup pure honey
   ¼ cup vegetable oil
   1 teaspoon pure vanilla extract
   1 egg
   ½ cup chopped unsalted walnuts
   ¼ cup sesame seeds

1. Preheat the oven to 375°F. In a large bowl, combine all ingredients; mix well.

2. On a floured surface, knead the dough until it is firm.

3. Roll the dough to a ½-inch thickness. Cut with the cookie cutter of your choice. Transfer cookies to a baking sheet.

4. Bake for 15 minutes. Turn off the heat; let the cookies stand in the oven until hard, 1 to 2 hours.

SESAME COOKIES

1½ cups whole-wheat flour
1 teaspoon baking powder
⅓ cup vegetable oil
¼ cup pure honey
1 egg
1 teaspoon pure vanilla extract
3 tablespoons sesame seeds

1. Preheat the oven to 375°F. In a large bowl, combine the flour, baking powder, oil, honey, egg, and vanilla; mix well.

2. On a floured surface, knead the dough until it is firm. Shape the dough into quarter-size balls.

3. Place the sesame seeds in a shallow bowl. Roll each dough ball in the sesame seeds, then flatten slightly. Place cookies on a baking sheet.

4. Bake for 10 to 15 minutes, or until the cookies are dry and firm to touch. Turn off the heat; let the cookies stand in the oven until hard, 1 to 2 hours.

APPLE AND PEANUT BUTTER TREATS

4 cups whole-wheat flour
¾ cup quick-cooking oats
¼ cup wheat germ
½ cup all-natural, unsweetened applesauce
½ cup all-natural peanut butter
(no sugar or salt added)
1½ cups water
2 teaspoons pure vanilla extract
1 egg

1. Preheat the oven to 350°F. In a large bowl, combine all ingredients; mix well.

2. On a floured surface, knead the dough until it is firm.

3. Roll the dough to a ¼-inch thickness. Cut with the cookie cutter of your choice. Transfer cookies to a baking sheet.

4. Bake for 45 minutes. Turn off the heat; let the cookies stand in the oven until hard, 1 to 2 hours.

VANILLA NUT TREATS

3 cups unbleached white flour
¼ teaspoon baking powder
½ teaspoon nutmeg
½ cup pure honey
½ cup vegetable oil
1 tablespoon skim milk
1 teaspoon pure vanilla extract
1 egg
½ cup chopped unsalted peanuts

1. Preheat the oven to 400°F. In a large bowl, combine all ingredients; mix well.

2. On a floured surface, knead the dough until it is firm.

3. Roll the dough to a ½-inch thickness. Cut with the cookie cutter of your choice. Transfer cookies to a baking sheet.

4. Bake for 10 minutes. Turn off the heat; let the cookies stand in the oven until hard, 1 to 2 hours.

SESAME CREAM CHEESE BISCUITS

2 cups whole-wheat flour
½ cup sesame seeds
½ cup vegetable oil
⅓ cup low-fat cream cheese, softened
¼ cup pure honey
½ teaspoon pure vanilla extract

1. Preheat the oven to 400°F. In a large bowl, combine all ingredients; mix well.

2. On a floured surface, knead the dough until it is firm.

3. Roll the dough to a ¼-inch thickness. Cut with the cookie cutter of your choice. Transfer cookies to a baking sheet.

4. Bake for 10 to 15 minutes, or until the cookies are dry and firm to touch. Turn off the heat; let the cookies stand in the oven until hard, 1 to 2 hours.

MOLASSES PEANUT TREATS

2 cups whole-wheat flour
1 cup quick-cooking oats
½ cup wheat germ
¾ cup water
½ cup chopped unsalted peanuts
1 tablespoon all-natural molasses

1. Preheat the oven to 350°F. In a large bowl, combine all ingredients until a firm dough forms.

2. On a floured surface, knead the dough until it is firm.

3. Roll the dough to a ¼-inch thickness. Cut with the cookie cutter of your choice. Transfer cookies to a baking sheet.

4. Bake for 20 minutes. Turn off the heat; let the cookies stand in the oven until hard, 1 to 2 hours.

PUMPKIN NUT BREAD

1 cup solid packed pumpkin
½ cup vegetable oil
¼ cup pure honey
1 egg
1½ cups whole-wheat flour
½ cup wheat germ
½ teaspoon baking powder
½ cup chopped unsalted peanuts
½ teaspoon ground cinnamon
½ teaspoon ground nutmeg

1. Preheat the oven to 350°F. Grease an 8½" x 4½" x 2¾" loaf pan.

2. In a medium bowl, combine the pumpkin, vegetable oil, honey, and egg; mix well.

3. In a large bowl, combine the flour, wheat germ, baking powder, peanuts, cinnamon, and nutmeg. Slowly add the wet ingredients to the dry mixture; mix well.

4. Pour the batter into the prepared pan.

5. Bake until a toothpick inserted in the center comes out clean, 55 minutes to 1 hour.

SUNFLOWER SEED THINS

½ cup chopped unsalted sunflower seeds
1 cup whole-wheat flour
¼ cup vegetable oil
1 tablespoon water

1. Preheat the oven to 350°F. Place the sunflower seeds on a baking sheet and toast until golden brown, 20 to 25 minutes.

2. In a medium-size bowl, combine the flour, oil, water, and toasted sunflower seeds.

3. Reduce heat to 300°F. On a lightly floured surface, knead the dough until it is firm. If the dough is too soft, chill it for a few minutes.

4. Roll the dough to a ⅛-inch thickness. Cut into rounds using a shot glass or round cookie cutter. Transfer the crackers to a baking sheet.

5. Bake for 30 minutes. Turn off the heat; let the crackers stand in the oven until hard, 1 to 2 hours.

WALNUT WAFERS

2 cups rice flour
1 tablespoon wheat germ
¼ cup pure honey
¼ cup vegetable oil
½ teaspoon pure vanilla extract
½ cup chopped unsalted walnuts
¼ cup sesame seeds

1. Preheat the oven to 375°F. In a large bowl, combine all ingredients.

2. On a floured surface, knead the dough until it is firm. Divide the dough into 6 equal parts.

3. Using your hands, roll each section of dough into a log shape. Wrap each log in wax paper and chill for 1 hour.

4. Cut the logs into ½-inch-thick slices. Transfer the cookies to a baking sheet.

5. Bake for 15 minutes. Turn off the heat; let the cookies stand in the oven until hard, 1 to 2 hours.

SUNFLOWER BISCUITS

  2¾ cups whole-wheat flour
  ½ cup unsalted sunflower seeds
  ¼ cup pure honey
  ¼ cup water
  2 tablespoons vegetable oil
  2 eggs

1. Preheat the oven to 350°F. In a large bowl, mix together all ingredients.

2. On a floured surface, knead the dough until it is firm.

3. Roll the dough to a ½-inch thickness. Cut with the cookie cutter of your choice. Transfer cookies to a baking sheet.

4. Bake for 30 minutes. Turn off the heat; let the cookies stand in the oven until hard, 1 to 2 hours.

Meat-Lovers Menu

Unlike commercial treats, which are often made with overprocessed bits and pieces of meat left over from other cuts, these biscuits and cookies are made with top-quality meat. They not only are healthier for your dog, but they taste better, too!

LIVER AND CHEESE BISCUITS

  3¼ cups whole-wheat flour
  1½ cups wheat germ
  ½ cup freeze-dried liver (available at health food stores)
  1 cup low-fat cottage cheese
  2 eggs

1. Preheat the oven to 300°F. In a large bowl, combine all ingredients.

2. On a floured surface, knead the dough until it is firm.

3. Roll the dough to a ½-inch thickness. Cut with the cookie cutter of your choice. Transfer biscuits to a baking sheet.

4. Bake for 1 hour, or until the biscuits are dry and firm to touch. Turn off the heat; let the biscuits stand in the oven until hard, 1 to 2 hours.

BEEF TREATS

    1 cup chopped lean beef
    2 cups unbleached white flour
    ½ cup wheat germ
    ¼ cup low-fat powdered milk
    ½ cup vegetable oil
    ½ cup water
    1 egg

1. Preheat the oven to 350°F. In a skillet, sauté the beef until cooked through. Drain thoroughly.

2. In a large bowl, combine all ingredients; mix well.

3. On a floured surface, knead the dough until it is firm.

4. Roll the dough to a ½-inch thickness. Cut with the cookie cutter of your choice. Transfer cookies to a baking sheet.

5. Bake for 30 minutes. Turn off the heat; let the cookies stand in the oven until hard, 1 to 2 hours.

LIVER AND OATS TREATS

Recommended safe amount: One treat per 2.7 lbs of body weight per day (see Garlicky Treats, page 16).

    1½ cups rice flour
    1½ cups whole-wheat flour
    1 cup rye flour
    1 cup quick-cooking oats
    ¼ cup liver powder (available at health food stores)
    1½ cups water
    ¼ cup vegetable oil
    1 egg
    1 clove garlic, minced

1. Preheat the oven to 325°F. In a large bowl, combine all ingredients; mix well.

2. On a floured surface, knead the dough until it is firm.

3. Roll the dough to a ½-inch thickness. Cut with the cookie cutter of your choice. Transfer cookies to a baking sheet.

4. Bake for 1 hour. Turn off the heat; let the cookies stand in the oven until hard, 1 to 2 hours.

CHICKEN AND CHEESE BISCUITS

 2 cups water
 1 chicken leg, skin and bones removed
 3 cups whole-wheat flour
 ½ cup shredded low-fat Cheddar cheese
 ⅓ cup vegetable oil
 1 egg

1. Pour the water into a small pan and set the chicken in it. Bring to a boil and simmer until the chicken is fully cooked, 10 to 15 minutes. Set the cooked chicken aside; reserve ¾ cup of the cooking liquid.

2. Preheat the oven to 350°F. In a large bowl, combine the flour, cheese, oil, and egg; mix well.

3. Shred the chicken meat; stir into the dough. Add the reserved cooking liquid; mix until completely combined.

4. On a floured surface, knead the dough until it is firm.

5. Roll the dough to a ½-inch thickness. Cut with the cookie cutter of your choice. Transfer the biscuits to a baking sheet.

6. Bake for 50 minutes. Turn off the heat; let the biscuits stand in the oven until hard, 1 to 2 hours.

CATCH OF THE DAY

Recommended safe amount: One treat per 2.7 lbs of body weight per day (see Garlicky Treats, below).

   3 **cups unbleached white flour**
   ½ **cup cornmeal**
   ½ **cup wheat germ**
   1 **cup water**
   ½ **cup vegetable oil**
   1 **can (6 ounces) tuna in water, drained, rinsed, and drained again**
   1 **clove garlic, chopped**

1. Preheat the oven to 350°F. In a large bowl, combine all ingredients.

2. On a lightly floured surface, knead the dough until it is firm.

3. Roll the dough to a ½-inch thickness. Use a fish-shaped cookie cutter (or whatever shape you prefer) to form cookies. Transfer the cookies to a baking sheet.

4. Bake for 30 minutes. Turn off the heat; let the cookies stand in the oven until hard, 1 to 2 hours.

Garlicky Treats

Garlic is one of the wonder herbs of the kitchen. It adds flavor and zest to recipes, and studies suggest that it aids in fighting infection. In the case of homemade dog treats, however, garlic must be recommended with caution: high amounts of garlic is known to cause Heinz body anemia in dogs.

In 2008, the National Academy of Sciences released a report, "Safety of Dietary Supplements in Horses, Dogs, and Cats," that states intake levels that are presumed safe based on available research data. For dogs, that amount is 25 mg per 1 lb of body weight. Here's what that means: an average clove of garlic is about 3000 grams, so while a 60-lb dog could safely consume 1500 mg of garlic (about half a clove), a 20-lb dog could safely consume only 500 mg (about one-eighth of a clove).

All the recipes in this section, plus any recipe in other sections that contain garlic, include a recommended safe amount based the dog's weight.

CHEESE AND GARLIC BITES

Recommended safe amount: One treat per 3.3 lbs of body weight per day.

    2 cups whole-wheat flour
    ½ cup shredded low-fat Cheddar cheese
    ½ cup vegetable oil
    1 clove garlic, crushed

1. Preheat the oven to 375°F. In a large bowl, combine all ingredients; mix well.

2. On a floured surface, knead the dough until it is firm. Chill dough for 30 minutes.

3. Roll the dough to a ½-inch thickness. Cut with the cookie cutter of your choice. Transfer cookies to a baking sheet.

4. Bake for 15 minutes. Turn off the heat; let the cookies stand in the oven until hard, 1 to 2 hours.

GARLIC'N OAT TREATS

Recommended safe amount: One treat per 3.3 lbs of body weight per day.

    4 cups whole-wheat flour
    1½ cups water
    1 cup quick-cooking oats
    ⅓ cup vegetable oil
    4 cloves garlic, chopped
    1 egg

1. Preheat the oven to 325°F. In a large bowl, combine all ingredients; mix well.

2. On a floured surface, knead the dough until it is firm.

3. Roll the dough to a ½-inch thickness. Cut with the cookie cutter of your choice. Transfer cookies to a baking sheet.

4. Bake for 50 minutes to 1 hour, or until the cookies are dry and firm to touch. Turn off oven; let the cookies stand in the oven until hard, 1 to 2 hours.

POTATO-GARLIC PANCAKES

Recommended safe amount: One treat per 3.3 lbs of body weight per day.

>   2 medium carrots, grated
>   1 large potato, grated
>   ¼ cup low-fat shredded Cheddar cheese
>   ½ cup unbleached white flour
>   ½ cup wheat germ
>   ¼ cup quick-cooking oats
>   1 teaspoon vegetable oil
>   1 egg
>   1 egg white
>   1 clove garlic, crushed

1. Preheat the oven to 450°F. Grease a baking sheet with vegetable oil. In a large bowl, combine all ingredients; mix well.

2. Using a tablespoon, form the mixture into small pancakes. Drop the pancakes about 2 inches apart on the prepared baking sheet. Spread each pancake into a circle about 2 inches in diameter.

3. Bake until the pancakes are golden brown, about 15 minutes. Store in an airtight container in the refrigerator.

MINT AND GARLIC–BROWN RICE BISCUITS

Recommended safe amount: One treat per 2.4 lbs of body weight per day.

>   2¾ cups whole-wheat flour
>   1 cup cooked brown rice
>   ½ cup water
>   3 tablespoons vegetable oil
>   3 tablespoons dried mint leaves
>   1 clove garlic, crushed

1. Preheat the oven to 350°F. In a large bowl, combine all ingredients; mix well.

2. On a lightly floured surface, knead the dough until it is firm.

3. Roll the dough to a ¼-inch thickness. Cut with the cookie cutter of your choice. Transfer the biscuits to a baking sheet.

4. Bake for 25 minutes. Turn off the heat; let the biscuits stand in the oven until hard, 1 to 2 hours.

HERB CRACKERS

Recommended safe amount: One treat per 3.3 lbs of body weight per day.

> 2 cups unbleached white flour
> 1 tablespoon cornmeal
> ½ teaspoon baking powder
> 1 cup skim milk
> ¼ cup vegetable oil
> ¼ cup grated Romano cheese
> 1 teaspoon dried basil
> 1 teaspoon dried parsley
> 1 clove garlic, chopped

1. Preheat the oven to 400°F. In a large bowl, combine all ingredients; mix until a firm dough forms. Chill the dough for 30 minutes.

2. On a floured surface, roll the dough to a ¼-inch thickness. Cut into squares. Transfer the crackers to a baking sheet.

3. Prick each cracker two or three times with a fork.

4. Bake for 10 to 15 minutes, or until the crackers are golden brown and dry to touch. Turn off the heat; let the crackers stand in the oven until hard, 1 to 2 hours.

Fruity Favorites

Dogs enjoy a surprising variety of fruit. When shopping, look for organic produce. These fruits will be free of pesticides and other substances that often cause allergic reactions in dogs — and people.

APPLE-OATMEAL COOKIES

    3 cups whole-wheat flour
    1 cup quick-cooking oats, uncooked
    1 cup hot water
    ¼ cup vegetable oil
    1 tablespoon pure honey
    1 egg
    ½ apple, peeled, cored, and grated

1. Preheat the oven to 325°F. In a large bowl, combine all ingredients; mix well.

2. On a floured surface, knead the dough until it is firm.

3. Roll the dough to a ¼-inch thickness. Cut with the cookie cutter of your choice. Transfer the cookies to a baking sheet.

4. Bake for 50 minutes. Turn off the heat; let the cookies stand in the oven until hard, 1 to 2 hours.

APPLE AND HONEY DELIGHT

    3 cups whole-wheat flour
    ½ cup all-natural, unsweetened applesauce
    ½ cup water
    2 tablespoons pure honey
    1 egg

1. Preheat the oven to 350°F. In a large bowl, combine all ingredients; mix well.

2. Knead the dough until it is firm.

3. Roll the dough to a ¼-inch thickness. Cut with the cookie cutter of your choice. Transfer the cookies to a baking sheet.

4. Bake for 45 minutes. Turn off the heat; let the cookies stand in the oven until hard, 1 to 2 hours.

BANANA OAT MUFFINS

1½ cups oat flour
1 cup unbleached white flour
1 cup quick-cooking oats, uncooked
2 teaspoons baking soda
¾ cup water
¼ cup pure honey
3 tablespoons vegetable oil
2 ripe bananas, mashed
1 egg

1. Preheat the oven to 425°F. Line a muffin pan with 10 paper liners.

2. In a large bowl, combine the oat flour, white flour, oats, and baking soda. In a medium bowl, combine the water, honey, oil, bananas, and egg.

3. Add the wet ingredients to the dry mixture, a little at a time, mixing well after each addition.

4. Spoon the batter into the muffin cups, filling each about three-quarters full.

5. Bake until a toothpick inserted in the center of a muffin comes out clean, 15 to 20 minutes.

CREAM CHEESE–APPLE SURPRISE

2 cups whole-wheat flour
1 small package (4 ounces) low-fat cream cheese
½ cup all-natural, unsweetened applesauce
½ cup vegetable oil
2 teaspoons pure vanilla extract

1. Preheat the oven to 350°F. In a large bowl, combine all ingredients; mix well.

2. On a floured surface, knead the dough until it is firm.

3. Roll the dough to a ½-inch thickness. Cut with the cookie cutter of your choice. Transfer the cookies to a baking sheet.

4. Bake for 20 minutes. Turn off the heat; let the cookies stand in the oven until hard, 1 to 2 hours.

ORANGE TREATS

1¾ cups unbleached white flour
½ cup wheat germ
½ cup pure honey
½ cup vegetable oil
2 tablespoons pure vanilla extract
1 egg yolk
¼ cup sesame seeds
2 tablespoons grated orange rind

1. Preheat the oven to 375°F. In a large bowl, combine all ingredients; mix well.

2. On a lightly floured surface, knead the dough until it is firm.

3. Roll the dough to a ½-inch thickness. Cut with the cookie cutter of your choice. Transfer the cookies to a baking sheet.

4. Bake for 13 minutes. Turn off the heat; let the cookies stand in the oven until hard, 1 to 2 hours.

LEMON VANILLA CRISP

3 cups unbleached white flour
½ cup wheat germ
½ cup pure honey
½ cup vegetable oil
½ cup all-natural, unsweetened applesauce
2 tablespoons grated lemon rind
2 tablespoons pure vanilla extract
1 egg

1. Preheat the oven to 400°F. In a large bowl, combine all ingredients; mix well.

2. On a floured surface, knead the dough until it is firm.

3. Roll the dough to a ½-inch thickness. Cut into squares or into shapes using the cookie cutter of your choice. Transfer the cookies to a baking sheet.

4. Bake for 10 minutes. Turn off the heat; let the cookies stand in the oven until hard, 1 to 2 hours.

Icy Delights for Hot Summer Days

When the heat of summer has your pooch drooping, try serving these frosty, refreshing ice crystals.

HONEYDEW ICE

 3 pounds honeydew melon
⅓ cup water
¼ cup pure honey
 1 tablespoon fresh lemon juice

1. Discard the rind from the melon. Cut the fruit into 1-inch chunks.

2. Combine the melon, water, honey, and lemon juice in a blender. Purée the mixture.

3. Pour the mixture into ice-cube trays. Freeze until solid. Transfer the ice cubes to resealable plastic bags.

4. To serve, place a few ice cubes in another resealable plastic bag and crush with a mallet or hammer. Then set out the crystals in a bowl.

FROSTY FRUIT-AND-NUT CUBES

 1 container (32 ounces) all-natural, low-fat vanilla yogurt
1½ ripe bananas, mashed
 2 tablespoons all-natural peanut butter (no sugar or salt added)
 2 tablespoons pure honey
½ cup carob chips (available at health food stores)

1. In a blender, combine the yogurt, bananas, peanut butter, and honey. Blend until smooth.

2. Add the carob chips; stir well.

3. Pour the mixture into ice-cube trays. Freeze until solid. Transfer ice cubes to resealable plastic bags.

4. To serve, place a few ice cubes in another resealable plastic bag and crush with a mallet or hammer. Then set out the crystals in a bowl.

Doggie Desserts

Dog treats are, after all, treats. These faux desserts will have your dog begging for more opportunities to sit up, lie down, and fetch — anything for the reward!

BEST-FRIEND BIRTHDAY CAKE

  2 cups unbleached white flour
  2 teaspoons baking powder
  1 teaspoon baking soda
  ¼ cup wheat germ
  ¾ cup water
  ¼ cup vegetable oil
  ¼ cup unsweetened applesauce
  1 egg
  ⅔ cup mashed bananas
  ½ cup carob chips (available at health food stores)

1. Preheat the oven to 350°F. Grease and flour an 8-inch square pan. In a large bowl, combine all ingredients; mix well.

2. Pour the batter into the prepared pan.

3. Bake until a toothpick inserted in the center comes out clean, about 25 minutes. Allow the cake to cool completely before frosting.

BIRTHDAY CAKE FROSTING AND GARNISH

  1 package (8 ounces) low-fat cream cheese, softened
  ¼ cup mashed bananas
  2 tablespoons pure honey
  1 tablespoon unbleached flour
  ½ cup carob chips (available at health food stores), chopped

1. In a medium-size bowl, combine the cream cheese, bananas, honey, and flour; mix until smooth. If the frosting is not firm, add more flour and continue mixing until firm.

2. Spread a thin layer of frosting on a cooled cake. Sprinkle carob chips over the frosting to decorate.

TEMPTING CHEESE CIRCLES

3 cups whole-wheat flour

1½ cups wheat germ

1 cup quick-cooking oats

1½ cups hot water

¼ cup vegetable oil

1 egg

¾ cup shredded low-fat Cheddar cheese

1. Preheat the oven to 300°F. In a large bowl, combine all ingredients; mix well.

2. On a floured surface, knead the dough until it is firm.

3. Using your hands, roll the dough into the shape of a log. Cut into even, ⅛-inch-thick slices. Transfer the slices to a baking sheet.

4. Bake for 1 hour. Turn off the heat; let the cookies stand in the oven until hard, 1 to 2 hours.

CAROB MINT DROPS

2 cups brown rice flour

⅔ cup water

3 tablespoons vegetable oil

1 large egg

½ cup carob chips (available at health food stores)

½ cup chopped parsley

⅓ cup chopped fresh mint

1. Preheat the oven to 350°F. In a large bowl, combine all ingredients; mix well. The mixture should be the consistency of dough for drop cookies; if it is too thick, add water.

2. Drop the dough by the teaspoonful, ½ inch apart, onto a baking sheet.

3. Bake for 15 minutes. Turn off the heat; let the cookies stand in the oven until hard, 1 to 2 hours.

BANANA OATMEAL BITES

 4 cups whole-wheat flour
 ½ cup quick-cooking oats
1¼ cups water
 2 tablespoons vegetable oil
 1 teaspoon pure vanilla extract
 1 egg
 1 small ripe banana, chopped
 ¼ cup carob chips (available at health food stores)

1. Preheat the oven to 350°F. In a large bowl, combine all ingredients; mix well.

2. On a floured surface, knead the dough until it is firm.

3. Roll the dough to a ½-inch thickness. Cut with the cookie cutter of your choice. Transfer the cookies to a baking sheet.

4. Bake for 30 to 45 minutes, or until the cookies are dry and firm to touch. Turn off the heat; let the cookies stand in the oven until hard, 1 to 2 hours.

CAROB ALMOND CRUNCH

1½ cups unbleached white flour
 ½ cup vegetable oil
 ¼ cup pure honey
 ½ teaspoon pure almond extract
 1 egg
 ½ cup carob chips (available at health food stores)
 ½ cup chopped unsalted almonds

1. Preheat the oven to 375°F. In a large bowl, combine all ingredients; mix well.

2. On a lightly floured surface, knead the dough until it is firm.

3. Roll the dough to a ½-inch thickness. Cut with the cookie cutter of your choice. Transfer the cookies to a baking sheet.

4. Bake for 10 minutes. Turn off the heat; let cookies stand in the oven until hard, 1 to 2 hours.

MILK AND HONEY DELIGHTS

3 cups whole-wheat flour
½ cup powdered skim milk
¾ cup water
¼ cup vegetable oil
1 tablespoon pure honey
1 egg

1. Preheat the oven to 325°F. In a large bowl, combine all ingredients; mix well.

2. On a floured surface, knead the dough until it is firm.

3. Roll the dough to a ½-inch thickness. Cut with the cookie cutter of your choice. Transfer the cookies to a baking sheet.

4. Bake 50 minutes, or until the cookies are dry and firm to touch. Turn off the heat; let the cookies stand in the oven until hard, 1 to 2 hours.

CAROB WALNUT TREATS

1 cup carob chips (available at health food stores)
2¾ cups whole-wheat flour
½ cup chopped unsalted walnuts
½ cup pure honey
¼ cup vegetable oil
¼ cup water
1 teaspoon baking powder

1. Place the carob in a double boiler set over low heat; stir until melted.

2. Using a spatula, scrape the melted carob into a large bowl and let it cool to room temperature.

3. Preheat the oven to 350°F. Add the flour, walnuts, honey, oil, water, and baking powder to the melted carob; mix well.

4. Divide the dough in half. Wrap each half in plastic wrap and chill until firm, about 1 hour.

5. On a lightly floured surface, roll the dough to a ¼-inch thickness. Cut with the cookie cutter of your choice. Transfer the cookies to a baking sheet.

6. Bake for 8 to 10 minutes, or until the cookies are dry and firm to touch. Turn off the heat; let the cookies stand in the oven until hard, 1 to 2 hours.

WHOLESOME HONEY TREATS

    2 cups rice flour
    2 cups unbleached white flour
    2 cups whole-wheat flour
    2 cups quick-cooking oats
    ½ cup wheat germ
    1¾ cups water
    ¾ cup low-fat milk
    ½ cup pure honey

1. Preheat the oven to 350°F. In a large bowl, combine all ingredients; mix well.

2. On a floured surface, knead the dough until it is firm.

3. Roll the dough to a ¼-inch thickness. Cut with the cookie cutter of your choice. Transfer the cookies to a baking sheet.

4. Bake for 30 to 45 minutes, or until the cookies are dry and firm to touch. Turn off the heat; let the cookies stand in the oven until hard, 1 to 2 hours.

GINGER COOKIES

    5 cups whole-wheat flour
    1½ tablespoons baking soda
    1 tablespoon ground ginger
    2 teaspoons ground cinnamon
    ¾ cup all-natural, unsweetened applesauce
    ¾ cup all-natural molasses
    ½ cup pure honey
    ¼ cup vegetable oil
    1 egg

1. Preheat the oven to 375°F. In a large bowl, combine all ingredients.

2. On a floured surface, knead the dough until it is firm.

3. Chill the dough for 1 hour.

4. On a floured surface, roll the dough to a ¼-inch thickness. Cut with the cookie cutter of your choice. Transfer the cookies to a baking sheet.

5. Bake for 7 minutes. Turn off the heat; let the cookies stand in the oven until hard, 1 to 2 hours.

MULTIGRAIN CHEESE BISCUITS

    3 cups whole-wheat flour
    1 cup quick-cooking oats
    1 cup cornmeal
    ½ cup low-fat powdered milk
    ½ cup wheat germ
    1½ cups water
    ¼ cup vegetable oil
    1 egg
    ½ cup shredded low-fat Cheddar cheese

1. Preheat the oven to 300°F. In a large bowl, combine all ingredients; mix well.

2. On a floured surface, knead the dough until it is firm.

3. Roll the dough to a ½-inch thickness. Cut with the cookie cutter of your choice. Transfer the biscuits to a baking sheet.

4. Bake for 1 hour. Turn off the heat; let the biscuits stand in the oven until hard, 1 to 2 hours.

CAROB AND OAT-NOLA BARS

    1 cup quick-cooking oats
    ¾ cup Oat-Nola (see recipe on page 30)
    ½ cup plus 1 tablespoon pure honey
    3 tablespoons vegetable oil
    1 egg
    ¼ teaspoon pure vanilla extract
    ¼ cup whole-wheat flour
    ½ cup carob chips (available at health food stores)

1. Preheat the oven to 325°F. Grease and flour an 11" x 7" baking sheet. In a large bowl, combine the oatmeal, Oat-Nola, and ½ cup of the honey. Pour in the oil; blend thoroughly.

2. In a medium-size bowl, combine the egg, vanilla, and remaining 1 tablespoon of honey; beat well.

3. Add the wet mixture to the oatmeal mixture. Add the flour and carob chips; stir until smooth.

4. Press the mixture evenly into the prepared baking sheet.

5. Bake for 35 minutes. Cool slightly and cut into bars of desired size.

OAT-NOLA

1½ cups quick-cooking oats
½ cup wheat germ
½ cup unsalted sunflower seeds
½ cup pure honey
2 tablespoons vegetable oil

1. Preheat the oven to 325°F. Grease a baking sheet. In a large bowl, combine all ingredients; mix well.

2. Spread the mixture onto the prepared baking sheet. Bake for 25 minutes; let cool.

3. Transfer the Oat-Nola to a resealable plastic bag and crush into smaller pieces.

CAROB CHIP BISCOTTI

3½ cups whole-wheat flour
½ teaspoon baking powder
½ teaspoon baking soda
½ teaspoon ground cinnamon
2 tablespoons vegetable oil
½ cup pure honey
3 egg whites
1 egg
1 teaspoon pure vanilla extract
1 teaspoon grated orange rind
½ cup carob chips (available at health food stores)

1. Preheat the oven to 375°F. In a large bowl, combine all ingredients.

2. On a lightly floured surface, knead the dough until it is firm. Divide the dough in half.

3. Place half of the dough on a baking sheet. Roll into a rectangle about 5 inches wide by 12 inches long. Repeat with second half of dough.

4. Bake the dough until a toothpick inserted in the center comes out clean, about 30 minutes.

5. Remove the baking sheet from the oven and cut the biscotti into slices, 1 inch wide by 3 inches long.

6. Return the baking sheet to the oven; turn off the heat and let the biscotti stand in the oven until hard, 1 to 2 hours.

OATMEAL–CAROB CHIP COOKIES

3¼ cups whole-wheat flour
2½ cups quick-cooking oats
½ cup wheat germ
1 cup water
¼ cup pure honey
¼ cup vegetable oil
¼ cup carob chips (available at health food stores)

1. Preheat the oven to 300°F. In a large bowl, combine all ingredients; mix well.

2. On a floured surface, knead the dough until it is firm. Chill dough for 30 minutes.

3. Roll the dough to a ½-inch thickness. Cut with the cookie cutter of your choice. Transfer the cookies to a baking sheet.

4. Bake for 1 hour. Turn off the heat; let the cookies stand in the oven until hard, 1 to 2 hours.

BRAN AND OATMEAL BITES

4½ cups whole wheat flour
½ cup no-sugar-added bran-flake cereal
½ cup quick-cooking oats
1 cup skim milk
¼ cup pure honey
2 eggs
¼ cup carob chips (available at health food stores)

1. Preheat the oven to 350°F. In a large bowl, combine all ingredients; mix well.

2. Knead the dough until it is firm.

3. Roll the dough to a ½-inch thickness. Cut with the cookie cutter of your choice. Transfer the cookies to a baking sheet.

4. Bake for 20 minutes. Turn off the heat; let the cookies stand in the oven until hard, 1 to 2 hours.

CARROT-YOGURT MUFFINS

1 container (8 ounces) plain low-fat yogurt
⅓ cup pure honey
3 tablespoons all-natural, unsweetened applesauce
3 carrots, grated
2 eggs
2 cups whole-wheat flour
½ cup wheat germ
1 teaspoon baking powder
1 teaspoon baking soda
½ cup chopped unsalted walnuts

1. Preheat the oven to 350°F. Line a muffin pan with 12 paper liners.

2. In a medium-size bowl, combine the yogurt, honey, applesauce, carrots, and eggs; mix well.

3. In a large bowl, combine the flour, wheat germ, baking powder, baking soda, and walnuts; mix well.

4. Add the wet ingredients to the dry mixture, a little at a time, mixing well after each addition.

5. Spoon batter into the muffin cups, filling each three-quarters full.

6. Bake until a toothpick inserted in the center of one comes out clean, about 18 minutes.

CONVERTING RECIPE MEASUREMENTS TO METRIC

Use the following chart for converting U.S. measurements to metric. Since these conversions are not exact, it's important to convert the measurements for all of the ingredients to maintain the same proportions as the original recipe.

To convert to	From	Multiply by
milliliters	teaspoons	4.93
milliliters	tablespoons	14.79
milliliters	fluid ounces	29.57
milliliters	cups	236.59
liters	cups	0.236
grams	ounces	28.35

To convert Fahrenheit to centigrade, subtract 32, multiply by 5, and divide by 9.